16,95

DON'T WORRY

DON'T WORRY

Geoff Hattersley

BLOODAXE BOOKS

ISBN: 1 85224 272 8

First published 1994 by
Bloodaxe Books Ltd,
P.O. Box 1SN,
Newcastle upon Tyne NE99 1SN.

Bloodaxe Books Ltd acknowledges
the financial assistance of Northern Arts.

*For Jeanette Hattersley,
my family and friends*

Cover printing by J. Thomson Colour Printers Ltd, Glasgow.

Printed in Great Britain by
Cromwell Press Ltd, Broughton Gifford, Melksham, Wiltshire.

Contents

II. ACT

III. DON'T WORRY

Acknowledgements

Acknowledgements are due to the editors of the following publications in which some of these poems first appeared: *Ambit, Bad Seeds, Brackenhall and Sheepridge Community Newsletter, Cabaret 246, Contraflow, Dog, The Echo Room, The Guardian, Harry's Hand, Joe Soap's Canoe, Jonathon, Klick, Krax, Label, The New Poetry* (Bloodaxe Books, 1993), *The North, Odyssey, Pennine Platform, Poetry with an Edge* (Bloodaxe Books, new edition, 1993), *Poesie Europe* (Germany), *Scratch, Slow Dancer, Stride, Sunk Island Review, Uncompromising Positions, Verse, West Coast Magazine* and *The Wide Skirt*.

Some of the poems in the first section, 'Because', or earlier versions of them, have also appeared in the following small press titles by Geoff Hattersley: *The Deep End* (Echo Room Press, 1987), *Slouching Towards Rotherham* (Wide Skirt Press, 1987, 1989), *Shadows on the Beach* (Red Sharks Press, 1987), *The New Right* (Smith Doorstop Books, 1987), *Port of Entry* (Littlewood Press, 1989), *Sex and other poems* (Smith Doorstop Books, 1990), *The Saxophonist's Eyes* (Echo Room Press, 1990), *The Good Stuff* (Wide Skirt Press, 1990). Some poems have been broadcast on BBC Radio 3 & 4.

I. BECAUSE

Because

Because his face did not fit
he walked in sideways, on his hands,
pushing a wheelbarrow loaded with groceries.

His moustache sweating, he pogo–danced the bump
toward the bowl of tulips, grabbed a bunch
and ate them noisily while whistling 'Little Stevie'.

He gave piggy–back rides to all the pregnant women.
He impersonated a trout on the end of a hook.
He applauded their insults

because his face did not fit.
And if it's true he didn't 'get the joke',
it's also true the joke wasn't very funny.

The Cigar

The cigar was huge. It was carried in
by three underfed slave-children in chains.

Everything stopped: spoons on their paths to mouths,
hands and feet meeting knees beneath tables.

The American glanced around slowly,
the beginnings of an imbecilic grin...

Before the cartoon gapes of the other customers,
he summoned a blow-torch and lit the thing.

It began to expand at an alarming rate,
taking a new, strange form, developing

what seemed to be a head. One woman abandoned
her life's jewellery, collapsed to the ground moaning

'Give it *me*! Give it *me*!' Her husband, tears streaming,
gobbled a photograph of their lovely children.

Chandeliers fell crashing; in the darkness,
bottles of wine ran back to the cellar,

remarkable creatures leapt from their plates,
forked just in time by the sweating manager.

Waiters, their bow-ties on the verge of hysteria,
rushed to and fro with bowls of hot veal soup.

The American celebrated loudly
by eating the whole five-pound lump

of garlic stilton with port wine on the dessert trolley.
The room was small and becoming increasingly

smaller. There seemed no escape

Boys' Grammar School: The New Boy Hears Good Advice in the Toilet

Sing heartily the morning hymns
but remember: God

is a mathematics master
known, secretly, as Boris.

And God is with you;
always

bolt the door
when you smoke in the toilet

for remember: God
shall punish his errant children.

And you shall meet God
and tremble before Him.

And God shall frown
and God shall shout

and God shall slam His fist
upon the polished table-top.

And God's cane shall cut
through air and laws,

His hard-on no secret,
except to His wife.

Factory, Late Seventies

1. *Foreman*

The foreman requires
that things run smoothly.
His ambition is to be
world champion of foremen.
He paces the factory floor,
checking, checking, offering
words of encouragement
or abuse here and there.

I'm busy twisting the screwdriver
into the shining face
of the instrument panel
when he surprises me,
voice low in my ear:
'I could sack you for this...'
Then walks away, whistling.

2. *Knife*

Don leans forward,
lights my cigarette
with a match snapped in half
between finger and thumb,
tries to interest me again
in the NF: 'Our meetings
are dead inspiring.'
He has a loud voice
with which to call me
a dif and wog-lover
and believes I've no sense
of reality. I watch him
scratching PAKIS GO 'OME
on the toilet wall,
turning suddenly he says
'I always carry a knife,
didn't you know that?'

3. *Hand*

It's pie, chips and beans
again in the canteen
as Sukdhev shows me the hand
crushed in the machine
I'm working with now.
You must, he says, be careful.

Ralph overhears, tells me later
about the compensation –
the new car and central heating,
the softer job, swears
it's true: 'Half the blokes
in the place have at least
one finger missing, look
if you don't believe me.
Lose an arm, you hit the jackpot.'

All day I pull the pipes
out from the presses
just in time. It's automatic,
you can't go wrong, can't
just close your eyes and think
what you'll do with the money

Split Shift

Everyone's reason
to smile: finished
for the day at two,

beer from ice-buckets
and music on the lawn
the whole afternoon.

I was working a split shift
in the kitchen, washing dishes
ten till two, five till eight.

The last thing I remember
is the sound of those dishes
hitting the ground outside

and the window,
one thin piece of glass
still tottering in the pane

like it's tempted
but can't quite allow
itself to fall.

The Joke

He's standing in the doorway
clutching his stomach.
He looks like any man
who's recently swallowed

a whole bottle of shaving foam
and doesn't know it.
We filled his mouth with it
last night at the party

after he'd fallen asleep
on the chair in the corner.
When we'd looked again, a little
later, the shaving foam

had gone, so we'd filled his mouth
again, and then again
till the bottle was empty.
It was a joke; we were all drunk.

Now in sunlight
he looks sadly at his stomach,
says he feels *a bit sick*,
and swears off alcohol.

Shadows on the Beach

On the beach at Dahab, the sand was hot.
It felt good to sit there, to be naked
and take things easy, to glance out to where
the women plunged shouting into the sea.
On the radio, Jim Morrison wanted
to be loved two times, Ba-by, loved twice today.

A small Bedouin girl approached,
a shadow on the pages of my book.
I looked up, smiled. Shyly, she asked
if she could eat the apple-core
I'd just dropped in the sand.

New Year's Morning

I came to under a bush in the park.
My watch had stopped at half-one and the face
was cracked. There were sharp pains in my chest as
I mounted the gate to get out of there.

There were chip-papers, discarded, there were
discarded chips and contraceptives. I
wasn't sure which town or city it was.
Whose mind had cracked open to reveal those

high-rise flats? I dodged back and then ran as
the police-car stopped and the door opened.
I hid in a yard, could hear the coppers
no more than a few feet away shouting

Where are you, you little bastard? They soon
got bored though and gave it up. A headache
hit me then. It was a New Year, alright,
but the old were most certainly still in.

There are other stories from those days too.

Love Poem

Alan hates John and Pete.
Pete hates Alan and John.
John hates Pete but not Alan.
I hate Pete and Alan

and John. Alan hates me.
Pete and John might hate me
for all I know. Nev hates
no one. No one hates Nev, though

the two boys from Dover
hate the lot of us. We hate
the two boys from Dover.
The two girls from Finchley

hate John and would hate Alan
too if they knew he read
their diaries. We all hate
the people we see with

money, the people who buy
groceries. The people
hate us also. I hate
the smell of France and its wine.

Theology

A good friend of mine
one day; the next,
someone who just happened
to look like her.

'God tapped me on the shoulder'
she said
and handed me the leaflet.

Returning home on the bus
I heard one schoolgirl
telling another
'Simon Bletsoe put his hand
on my fanny last night.'

Later, the same one
tapped me on the shoulder
to ask for a light.

Loomings, 1984

The future is a short journey by car
into a deep blue darkness –

such things will be common,
the pub comedians doing their best:

'A funny thing happened
on the way to Nottingham...'

I will be a broken radio
at the bottom of a filled-in mine-shaft,

all that will be left
of the village.

Shoulders

It was sad, as fathers and sons
who can't or won't speak
are sad, and I can't forget his face.

'No no no no'
was all he said, and then
'no no no no.'

He turned away
sharply and I stood
just a little behind

those broad, shaking shoulders,
useless
as a dead father to a live son.

Moon

The psychological need
for the drinking binge:
if you never let go,
how could you hold on?

Oh God give me the mind
of a moth, flying
inane circles
around my light-bulb,

give me the instincts
of an alligator, the humour
of a hyena, the anger
of a tea-drinking chimpanzee.

This is the quandary
of the young and foolish
as they begin to grow old:
there are, when you get down to it,

just two types of people alive,
those who have danced
beneath a full moon
and those who never have.

I would rather be a prisoner
than a prison-warder.
I would rather refuse a handout
than accept one.

I would like to live
at the bottom
of a swimming-pool,
the deep end.

He Was Certainly an Intellectual

He'd be there, poised with red pen
over the latest collection of Steiner essays,

eager to underline
everything obvious to you or me.

He liked to talk about famous literary figures:
Lawrence, Hardy, Eliot, Conrad, James –

they were all such wonderful people
who'd done such wonderful things.

He could talk for hours and hours.
Hadn't he written twenty-two hundred

letters over the years to *The Observer*?
Hadn't he read *Heart of Darkness*

seventeen times?
He could assure you he had.

The New Right

We tied him to a chair in a dark cellar
and pumped in water up to his chin.
After three days we drained the water
and revived him with a course of electric shocks.

For his own good.

We removed his fingernails and teeth
and drilled holes in his face. He needed a meal
so we force-fed him rusty nuts and bolts.
We beat the soles of his feet with golf-clubs.

For his own good.

We made him clean out the toilets with his beard.
We sawed off his left leg. He looked bored
so we hired a musician who entertained him
playing flute on his hollowed-out tibia.

For his own good.

We put a live eel inside his anus and fed
his genitals to a rat. We stuck needles in his eyes.
We cut off his nipples with a pair of rose-clippers
and dipped his tongue in paraffin and set fire to it.

For his own good.

With the aid of a suction-pump we removed his brain
through his ears and replaced it with mud.
We shot him at point-blank range five times
in the chest and six times in the head.

For his own good.

Sex

I admit it freely:
I was sulky for a while,
turning up to parties
wearing the face Elvis sported
the day Priscilla slammed the door,

the face Nixon hid behind
in the summer of '73. Or
was it '74? Whichever,
there were some neat card-tricks
and a presidential pardon,

nonsense for posterity:
A new type of hairstyle
will be proposed at ten p.m.
Thank you, you may switch off
the tape machine.

Now I remember:
I was seventeen, a bad year
whatever face I pull at it,
my first job
leading to my second and third

and fourth, none of them
anything
but spit on the head.
Then there was the sex thing.
We don't talk about sex.

That Weekend, You Wore

a tragic expression and were
loaded with meaningful glances.

We walked along the beach whipped
by sand on the wind, poked
at crabs half-eaten by gulls

and later, on the boating lake,
lost the oars and were forced
to abandon ship in the high wind.

There had to be a toilet
somewhere, but we couldn't find it,
so you disappeared into a bush,

and an old man's eyes grew wide
as he hobbled by – my clothes
dripping wet, a bent fag in my lips,

murmuring sweet nothings to a bush.

Portrait

'God I just love
your face' she says.

I'm sitting still
as she draws me,

trying to think
of something other

than how my arse
is killing me.

'Be patient your face
is a bastard

God I love it
I just love it!'

When the portrait
is done I might

carry it with me
in an inside

jacket pocket,
looking at it

occasionally
to see who I am.

Mucky

She puts down the magazine
and says she needs a bath,
looking at me as though
I do too or perhaps
only wanting me there with her

whether I'm mucky or not.
She's read 'The Platonic Blow'
(attributed to Auden)
just now and shows the face
that makes me grin and want

to hold her and startle her
with something of my own.
How mucky could I be? I
wonder, as the water
flows and the mirror steams.

Sheep's Brain

She tells me she once ate
a sheep's brain – now

here's me, with my tongue
halfway down her throat.

Half-Time

My main concern for the moment is me,
how I know food without sniffing at it,
know newspapers without picking them up,
how I can't even say the word *bathroom*
in anything other than a whisper.

Don't tell me it's not real, all that stuff
about heroic flights to distant stars
and pressing the ejector-button *just in time*.
It's real as this plate of chips, this sausage.
My best friends are all unemployable.

Hours

They drove the tanks over the barricades
and shot at anything moving
and I remembered:
A smoked mackerel salad
must be prepared for six o'clock.

Hours became neat words
and acts of love
and they poked long batons
into the prisoners' gunshot wounds
causing them to scream constantly.

Frank O'Hara Five, Geoffrey Chaucer Nil

I think on the whole I would rather read
Frank O'Hara than Geoffrey Chaucer, and
this fine, non-smoking morning could well be
the right time to try out a new (uh hum)

poetic form. It's the funniest thing:
I am *here*, thirty years of age, having
put booze and all sorts of, say, 'dubious
substances' behind me, now sweating it

all out in a small, constipated room
with a plump tomato of a woman,
conjugating Middle English verbs. I have
developed a line, a very brief line,

in gestures of friendliness, and in my
trousers an idea is taking shape.

Carte Blanche

Am I a person given to buffoonery?
A foolish jester? In short, a half-wit?

Am I a poor clown, awkwardly mimicking
the chief clowns in shows? Am I Merry Andrew?

These days my life is a sales campaign
conducted from a position of severe disadvantage

and the whole world's ambition
is to offer me shitty advice.

The only words I can think of
to describe my situation

are 'zany'
and 'sleep-needy'

and they are the wrong words
– believe me, Mac! 'Zany'

and 'sleep-needy'
are completely the wrong words.

I'm Putting On Weight, Last Year's Trousers

I give to my younger brother. He makes
some witty remark concerning those old
Orson Welles' wine adverts, and I tell him
Orson had been a genius, once, too.
Meanwhile, I suppose my ambition
(if I'm to be honest about it) is
to be paid to make those adverts. Fat chance.

Within These Walls

The revolution is but
a matter of days away
and dust settles on my
shelves and sleeping cat.
I'm a hundred miles from
where I was last week yet
this seat I'm sitting in looks
for all the world like
the same seat. Yesterday
I told my parents I'd
found a job and they
thought it a joke. It
was. The self-portrait
I have daubed, I call
'Still Life'.

Worksongs

Sober at last,
and on a day like this.
But to go back to what
I was saying last night:
Would you kill the bosses,
given half a chance
and a cast-iron alibi?

*

The woman in the canteen
saw me from a passing bus
at the crossroads in Bradley
on Saturday with my wife.
She holds up an almost
empty jar of Nescafé
like it was a death threat –
'I only bought it yesterday,
it cost four pounds thirty-nine.'
The first cup of the day is free.

*

I'm in charge
of my own room,
the others in it
do as I say,
if they know what's

Actually, they do
as they like,
which suits me fine,
though the boss
takes me aside:
'You're in charge
of this room, this machine.
Lay the law down,
lay the bloody
law down.'

*

The machine won't work
and I must make it.
I know less about it
than I do the temperature of rocks
in the Negev desert.
I know less about it
than I do the psychological needs
of tropical fish.
'What's the problem?'
the boss asks, poking
his nose round the door.
'The water molleton roller,
it needs replacing.'
It ought to fool him
at least another week.

*

The machine, the machine,
the bloody machine.
If I close my eyes
I see the machine.
If I open my eyes
I see the machine.
If I lick my lips
I taste the machine.

*

To call this living
is to call the ceiling sky,
the bathtub ocean.

At the end of each shift
and when I arrive the next morning
the place still stands.

I clear my head
of everything but the job,
decide the day's goal.

This day
that could have gone
anywhere.

Christmas Shopping, Sheffield

You were writing dud cheques
like no one's business,
I was splashing
the forged tenners around.

In the Hole in the Road
someone sang
'Take Me To Tulsa',
snow settling on his sombrero.
I tossed him a tenner
screwed into a ball.

A woman approached
armed with documents
and truth;
she was selling badges,
a definite bargain
at a tenner apiece.

I signed the petition
to end Apartheid,
I do a lot
of possibly useless writing.

It's Sunday

The man across the road
paints his drain-pipe bright red

while his wife holds the ladder
and Jimmy Saville recalls 1982

in short blurts of sap
that run into each other

to form one long blurt.
The corners of his mouth

dripping from the edge of his chin
the old boy next door

hands me a letter marked URGENT
delivered by mistake to him

three months ago.
Someone starts to mow his lawn

and then a couple of others
put on their oldest clothes too

and it's like a benevolent mental disease:
pretty soon, half the neighbourhood

are mowing their lawns in the sunshine
that glints blandly on row upon row

of identical rooftops and windows.

The Man at Number Ten

slams his front door:

there goes a man who
takes himself seriously,

shoulders hunched
for passers-by,

always busy
going nowhere, fast.

He spends every Sunday
with his head in an engine

and every single evening
throwing darts at a board.

He seems content
with a dog and a wife

and I've sometimes seen him
take one or both for a walk.

Almost Unbelievably

Sad, to be sitting here still
smoking too many cigarettes,
watching this cold pancake of a film
for the third time in one life,

to consider my mother,
patiently sitting through Western
after Western with my father
because she *liked the scenery*.

History repeats itself, after
a fashion, and these also
are facts: the diaries we've kept
would make appropriate palimpsests,

our stamp collection
ranks among the dull.
When the toast caught fire
last night and the grill,

it was the most exciting event
here for at least three years.

Future Games

(for Peter Sansom)

In summer and autumn
the kids spent the evenings

racing skateboards downhill
to the river. Now in winter

they find pleasure or pain indoors.
The suits their dads go drinking in,

the cars left standing in the rain,
show the sort of money

available – what seems
a never-ending pile.

Soon they'll make a sort of progress,
shuffling to interviews

that will become concerns,
jokes told over half-pints

that will last half the night
– as the glasses empty

they will too, into years
that get harder.

They won't ever feel powerful,
won't be.

They'll fit locks and raise dogs
to keep each other out,

they'll watch the river get
dirtier, deadlier.

They'll stop and gawp
at the sculpture

in memory
of the swimmers of '96.

Ear and throat infections
will be common killers.

Singing

Everybody's singing, they call it that.
In the bath, in the kitchen, in the car
on the way to work. And what do they sing?

They sing, Ooh Ba-by, let me feel your love.
They sing, Ooh Ba-by, need you're-las-tic-lips.
They sing, Ain't ea-sy for no man a-lone.

Everyone, in their cars, bathrooms, kitchens
– singing, singing. This is happiness, here.

The Drummer

He claimed to be a drummer
just a drummer

though we couldn't help but notice
the sticks in his hands, the obscenity

the way he'd stare, stare
ahead as he drummed

disturbing with his drums
his *drumming* the neighbourhood

stirring up things, things
best left unstirred, yes

at times *directly polemical*
this this this this drummer.

We could break his hands
and we did break them.

Briefcase

Life makes as much sense to me
as a ripe avocado does to a dog:
I was passed an unsigned cheque
by a man impersonating a friend

and got back home to a cold meal.
I found a man's black leather briefcase
in the corner of the bedroom
and knew it was my own.

How She Puts It

'It's about time you grew up' she says,
as though he doesn't know that theory.

'All I said' he starts to say
but she's not interested

in all he said, slamming
the door as she leaves.

He's both feet on her coffee table
when she later tells him it's over:

'Get out and take your ugliness with you'
is how she puts it.

The Saxophonist's Eyes

turn to the
doorway slowly

where two old drunks
are denying everything

then back to where
they found the music.

One drunk spills
his false teeth:

a quick wipe on a leg
they're in again.

Scared

He knows he's done wrong but wrong was done to him too.
In the first place his father read *The Lone Ranger*
to him each night as he masturbated.
His penis loathed itself. All his classmates
used to hang their coats and caps on his hook.

It didn't stop there. His first gun back-fired.
He was trying, it's true, to kill himself.
The woman happened to be in the way.
Then he got scared and things got out of hand.
The plane leaves in one hour thirty minutes.

Desert

We were out in the desert, just sort of
fooling around, dreaming up names for some
loud, long-haired rock band we'd be sure to form
the minute we got back home. I liked most

Doctor Straight Neck and his Toothpick Killers.
That was when Heidi started laughing and
couldn't stop – as much the drink and heat as
the wit, I guess. But it was good, hearing

her laugh like that, after the rape and all.
The desert could do that. Such stillness there,
as if the earth was taking breath, as if
history was yet to be invented.

I look after cacti in the house now.
They don't take much of that. I never did
keep in touch with any of those people,
though I heard Heidi died in Berlin, smack.

Snowballs, Italy

The Italians had received a tip-off:
on the border with France
a long line of traffic stretched back

through the deep, still-falling snow
like a black studded belt
across folds of white flesh.

I was sweating things out on the bus
among tattooed French and Dutch racists
when torchlight shook me up further.

We stood shivering by the road-side
as they emptied our bags brusquely one by one.
I needed a bath, I think people could tell.

As we left in the poor light
I watched young, bullet-shaped policemen
throwing snowballs at each other, laughing.

Spider

The spider was completely unprepared
for assault from above by an ash-tray,
it never had a friend it could count on.
It never knew its blood-group.
It never saw itself changing, or any need to.
It never said: 'No more excuses.'
It never felt tempted by drugs.
It never knew the itch to the nearest bar.
Its earning power was never an issue.
It was never hurt by a few home-truths.
It never did anything for anyone.
It never knew the myth of Wyatt Earp.
It never hoped for more than was likely.
It never had Watchtower thrust at it.
It never saw a rainbow, or a bunch of flowers
dropped into an open grave.
It never wrote an essay on the works of Alexander Pope.
It never filled in an application form.
It never married for love or money.
It never had a honeymoon in a hotel.
It never knew who was Prime Minister.
It never knew if it was lucky or not.
It never shopped for clothes.
It never smiled.
It never felt like a paperclip
in a jar in a cupboard in a shed.
It never carried a briefcase.
It never missed the last train.
It never slept off a hangover.
It never thought it was Marlon Brando.
It never grew a beard, or shaved in cold water.
It never fished in the Mississippi.
It never heard rumours about itself.
It never had to face its inadequacy.
It never had any wild ideas.
It never had any wild ideas drummed out of it.
It never laughed at a copper's helmet.
It never gave a false name and address.
It never saw The Marx Brothers, or listened to Sgt. Pepper.

It never knew what was in fashion.
It never got careless, or said it was past caring.
It never left its clothes lying in a heap.
It never preferred to remain anonymous.
It never wondered who wrote Shakespeare
or invented light-bulbs.
It never thought it would win an award one day.
It never moved because it didn't like the neighbourhood.
It never fastened its seat-belt for a rough ride.
It never played a guitar that had just one string.
It never looked for warts in its armpits.
It never turned its back on the dreams of its youth.
It never felt guilty for wasting time.
It never considered circumcision.
It never got hard-ons travelling by bus.
It never got sentimental at Christmas.
It never thought the carpet and curtains clashed.
It never spent a night awake with its partner
wishing the photograph album empty.
It never read about itself on the front page.
It never had more than its fair share of problems.
It was never diagnosed manic-depressive.
It was never found guilty of a thing.
It never made a list of things to do.
It never waited for the right partner to come along,
or became half of a couple with a headache between them.
It never dropped earwax in the ashtray.
It never had a first at the races.
It never tied a donkey to someone sleeping.
It never had a pension plan.
It never wanted to impress itself,
or thought it was better than it was.
It never got serious over the funniest things.
It never had a boss for a friend,
or a friend who thought he was a boss.
It never stared out to sea, it never watched the tide come in.
It never worried whether or not it created a good impression.
It never took notice of a roadsign.
It never put a barbed-wire fence up.
It never wept inside headphones, briefly.
It never learned to think things over more,
to peep before it plunged.

It never took its shoes off to save the carpet.
It never learned to spell archaeologist.
It never scratched its arse in a food-queue.
It never read a book about Hitler.
It never met a neo-oligarch.
It never used washing powder, or learned to start a fire.
It never used a telephone-box.
It never accepted a cigarette.
It never laughed at its own joke.
It never sat in the back row,
or dreamt it was the steering-wheel through James Dean's chest.
It never grew its hair to its shoulders.
It never picked its feet on the bed.
It never had a twenty-first birthday party.
It never washed its hands of anybody.
It never needed an explanation, or a diet.
It never said: 'Too gentle for my liking, too jolly.'
It never taught itself German, telling its partner
to be quiet so it could concentrate.
It never worried about what it was swallowing.
It never looked for heroes and villains.
It never smiled apologetically.
It never pressed a blade into its wrist.
It never wished it lived in a caravan.
It never fried bacon and eggs.
It never felt like a fat catalogue
of books published in limited editions
no one wants anyhow, not at any price.
It never tore a book in half.
It never felt like it was an abstract
that has everybody shaking their heads.
It never had a gun held to its head.
It never felt a wire tightened round its throat.
It was completely unprepared
for assault from above by an ashtray.
I should blush and compose
a relevant soundtrack for that moment.

Acknowledgements

are due to the following magazines/periodicals,
where some of these poems first appeared:

Ambidexterous Testicles; *The Bleeding Hearts'
Journal*; *Colonel Colonel*; *The Dog's Dinner*;
Excuse Me, I Have A Contagious Disease; *The
Frozen Foreskin*; *Gross Spinach*; *High Dive*;
Ink On Paper; *Jack's Journal*; *Kernel Kernel*;
Loincloth; *Melville's Dark Anus* (US); *Not The
Rialto*; *Oh! My Blue Hat*; *Poetry*; *Poetry* (US);
Poetry Now; *Poetry Today*; *Poetry Tomorrow*;
Poetry Yesterday; *Poetry Last Week But One*;
Poetry Please; *Poetry Scarborough* (US);
Quintessential Verse; *Reasonable People*;
The Slouch; *Time Gentlemen Please*; *Underbelly*;
Vaccinations Quarterly; *Writing Men*; (WHOOPS!);
Xenophobia (US); *Yelling Yowza* (US); *Zak's* (US);
Zee (US); *Zing* (US); *Zong* (US).

Some of the poems are reprinted from the pamphlets
Eating Sawdust With Willie (Close To God Books),
The Thinking Man's Thug (Stuffed Turkey Press),
Do Car-Workers Dream of Moving Pavements? (The
Under Duress Press), and *I Am The Man Who Used
To Hold The Dead* (The Dubious Usher Press).

II. ACT

Act

It was a normal day, raining
as he walked to the off-licence,
and there wasn't a bone in his body
someone wouldn't like to break
like a twig beneath the wheels of a slow train
or like a boiled egg brought down hard on a steel plate.

He'd thought his act had been simple;
clearly it hadn't been simple enough.
It's true some of the jokes were in bad taste
('the headless French horn player' springs to mind)
and some were hardly jokes at all – at least,
there's no point telling them if people can't get them.

One thing: he'd found out who his friends weren't.
He wouldn't want it any other way.

They'd packed him into a small suitcase.
What hadn't fit had been left at the station.

Slaughterhouse

At last, I was ready to say goodbye
to a tether made of fishnet stockings.
My friends told me not to, that I needed
a bandage for my head, needed a crutch for it.
I muttered Jolly Good like a jolly fellow,
caught the next bus. When I got where it was going
a man tried to sell me a Coke for five dollars.
I asked the next for the way to the slaughterhouse.
He told me to follow the smell of meat and bone.
The smell was powerful, at some distance even.

*

The first time I ate grilled octopus tentacles
– a strange moment, one I feel a need to mention.
An undercover cop had leeched onto me at a bar,
between mouthfuls of ouzo and tentacles
was pretending to be the greatest punk rock band ever.
He asked if I wanted to dance, the meathook
in my hand was reassuring. He loved every minute
of his pathetic life. Young men with sticks
surrounded our piled-high table
after he told the barman he should fuck his bill.

*

The morning after I ate grilled octopus tentacles
a man helped me buy powder in the pharmacy,
took me by the arm and found me a hotel room.
I was embarrassed among strangers the rest of the day
– they were passing round photos taken on the beach
that summer I weighed fifteen and a half stone.
At night I searched every room in the place,
sifting through bins stuffed with used tampons and shit-roll
for one small thing that would let me know where I was.
The landlady joined me about half-two.

*

I did press-ups and pull-ups and ran on the spot.
I brushed my teeth and shaved away three months
of enthusiastic cunnilingus.

I practised speaking without using shit and fuck
and held myself erect. Bumping into her on the stairs
I complimented her on her repertoire
but suggested she make more of a noise.
What do I most wish now, as I pick my teeth here
some years later? That she had understood a word I said
and that my nose hadn't been so obviously running.

*

The slaughterhouse started my head pounding
and there is a harsh sound, a hundred cows
screaming in unison. I went nuts there
and then. Years of treatment would have followed
if I hadn't escaped the building that minute.
I hitched a lift with a man who told me
I had good legs, sexy legs. He needed glasses
and a room at a hotel, I replied
– did he have his wallet? Yes he did. His head cracked
as he landed in the road, I didn't look back.

*

What I fell in love with was her singing,
not that it was what you'd call good singing.
It would reach me in my room as I lay naked
in the baked afternoons, talking aloud
to the insects on the ceiling and walls.
It was the happiness that surprised me,
and how it lingered a long time after.
I was never a music critic, no,
Not bad, I'd say, turning this way and that,
looking in the mirror at my pale face.

Untitled, Kibbutz, Late Seventies

He went round the dining room collecting
the unfinished bottles of sabbath wine
like a parody of Chaplin's drunken waiter
with a tray he somehow balanced just right.
And drank three half-pint glasses of vodka

and three bottles of beer in six minutes.
And collapsed, people dancing over him
as if he was a discarded jacket.
Then found himself acting the lumberjack,
singing at the top of his voice as the trees fell.

The Committee decided he wasn't dangerous
but resolved to keep a close watch on him.
He felt like he was a new species at a zoo.
He turned up to dinner disguised as Yassar Arafat,
reappeared the next day at the wedding party

as a rabbi who went round sniffing pants,
peeing where he felt like it, in front of the bride even,
and terrorised elderly guests
throughout the night, marching along their porches,
all Hitler moustache, goose-steps and salutes.

The Committee decided to give him a chance, another one.
He felt like he was bleeding to death in a stadium
with a capacity crowd having paid to watch.
He went to work with a swastika inked on his forehead.
He attacked a crippled war hero with a sweeping brush.

The Committee decided he deserved a chance.

The Fat Man in Paris

In the cafés and bars are all my friends.
I'm paying for all the drinks, everything.
What do I need money for if not friends?
What do I need friends for? There is no friend:
I've been through it, she says, I've had enough.

Let me tell you about the man who watches me.
He's sipping water at the bar in Jamaica.
He's on the beach in his suit in Miami.
Now we're in Paris; he watches, follows.
He knows I know, wants me to know.

A lizard by the bathroom door
stares as I dress. The girl's dressed already.
Take the whole five hundred, I say,
you've earned it. She says, God knows that.
I stop dressing and she leaves quietly.

Stinking leather boots, stinking leather pants.
I phone California, wanting to talk.
Needing to, but it's hard, it's John.
I am bloated, ugly, friendless, dying,
filling the bath with my vomit and unguents.

The man who watches me, who follows me,
he's across the road from the telephone,
he's talking with Customs at the airport.
He's running to keep up with the taxi,
taking it in his stride like a soldier.

The weight on my chest, the noise in my head.
Please god fuck my head for good completely.
Paris is an open prison, clever, clever.
The human race is one pair of scared eyes.
I see it coming, embrace it, so cold.

Pieces for Three Wooden Blocks

1

He won't go out the house
if a car's parked in front of it.
Instead he skulks in the cellar
where a pan collects rainwater
which he pours down the sink
each morning. He wears dark glasses
the whole time, even when shaving
in the mirror that needs cleaning.
A radio programme has to be taped
but there's no one he can trust to do it.

2

He sits quiet as an empty umbrella-stand.
He's closed the curtains and left the lights off.

He knows his enemies won't let it drop:
They'll stick his head on a pole, dance round it.

He's closed the curtains and left the lights off.
He thinks of a room with a door with no handle.
*

They'll stick his head on a pole, dance round it.
He should have listened to what friends told him.

He thinks of a room with a door with no handle.
He'd like that room. He'd like that door a lot.

He should have listened to what friends told him:
You go there with that face you can expect trouble.
*

He'd like that room, he'd like that door. A lot.
The thing he just can't get out of his head's

You go there with that face you can expect trouble.
Nothing's a joke, nothing's funny, nothing.

The thing he just can't get out of his head's
he knows his enemies won't let it drop.

Nothing's a joke, nothing's funny, nothing.
He sits quiet as an empty umbrella-stand.

3

He wondered what he'd see outside the car
and not from the seat where his legs were limp,
as though he'd walked a great distance or up
some flights of stairs, his thighs aching. He looked
out at the men and women, the women
more than the men, the way they stood, heads back
at the roadside. It seemed less of an illusion
now it was no longer what he'd see. What he'd see
too soon and for ever was something else.
He didn't want his eyes to water, but they did.

The Bootleg Series

He was still raving about Dylan's
The Bootleg Series months later.
He'd had his season in Hell
though the devil still visited
from time to time in the form
of sounds from the street.

His ex would call on Saturdays,
drop off their daughter. He'd play
The Bootleg Series and try
to get Christine to eat something.
She was between one and a half and two.
It's a funny age to be,

a funny one to watch.
She cheered him up when the grilling
he'd had from the detectives
started to get him down,
remembering the ice-bath.
The Bootleg Series cheered him up too.

The Bootleg Series was playing
the day the lawyer's letter came
telling him to forget it,
he was in poverty and would be
as long as his name wasn't
formerly Robert Allen Zimmerman,

The Bootleg Series his latest release,
bringing together strands
from a brilliant thirty-year career
– Christine could even dance
to parts of it, danced her dolls too
and joined in here and there.

So he traded in his mouth organ
for a fountain pen and got a job
writing job applications for people
who couldn't write their own
for some reason. He'd have gone nuts
it it wasn't for *The Bootleg Series*.

The year went past uneventfully.
His nails grew again,
his only pleasures in life
were *The Bootleg Series* and beer.
He put a little weight on,
took lessons in opening his mouth

without offending someone.
Christmas was a bastard of course,
but by the New Year he was
fully re-charged, ready to move.
He packed *The Bootleg Series*,
took a boat and finished up

eating pizza at a table
by the Med. *The Bootleg Series*
found new fans in the soldiers
who visited him in the room
where he cut the deals. He made
a killing and got out quick,

bought a house with the profits
in the remotest place he could think of.
Things drifted in and out of favour,
he found God, then lost Him,
but never at any point stopped
listening to *The Bootleg Series*.

You're Not Even Funny, Not Even Smart

Responsibilities, I collect them,
trying to bring you to your senses my latest.
Nobody knows what you've been through
and you'll keep it to yourself a while yet.
You sweat behind the bolted door, the cops
have twenty guns pointing at it, you've got
to open it, walk out. You finger your rifle
and weigh up the options and there are none.
Come in, you say, I've been expecting you.

Like I'm trapped in a phone box with a smell
I stand in your room and think *money back*.
You kick out your leg and the door closes
like a ton of rock, like a thousand tons.
You sit down, cross your feet at the ankles.
Sit down, you say, indicating a stool.
I think how sick you look, how very sick
as you suck that thermometer, dribbling.
You aren't dead but your room smells worse than it ought to.

You wanted all the things you thought you'd never want.
And stood aside, like a cardboard figure
let the other man push right in, the one
with bacon fat sticking to his front teeth.
He loved winding you up, you're so easy.
You're not even funny, not even smart
he told you in the rain, and he was right.
You're as good as dead, already buried, he said.
There's one in every town, you're it in ours.

How was it? Their endearments made you sick,
the love-making all but finished you off?
You shouldn't have been under the mattress.
I've read your notes, they're daft, obscene.
I don't know what you expected.
Now you tell yourself you don't care
and the funny thing is you don't, do you?
I look at your petulant mouth
and want to drag you outside by the hair.

Problems with the Overflow

You don't like to lose your cool and you don't
often. If you do, you think of a machine
that moves through the streets chopping legs off at the knees
and now the kids on the corner whistle
the funeral procession as you pass them.
But you're pretty thick-skinned and can take it
and there's always something to keep you from brooding:
a door that won't open or a door that won't close,
an overflow that keeps overflowing
or signs of strength or weakness in a rival.
What do you care if someone else freezes
in a bath they should have emptied?
You listened through the wall as he sang: he was deep
as a country 'n' western compilation
and with the same belief in the double-negative,
crackling like a 78 when he should have been a CD.
If his future was a building it would be demolished
but it's nothing to you since you woke up
and lit a fire - not a large one, about
the size of a copper's helmet or head.

Not far from where you spit, a family play
croquet on the lawn. There's a bright steel skateboard
poking under their gate like a machine.

Domestic

A shame the windows jammed, so the house smells
of paint and turps, some other stuff. But it looks great
from the end of the path or the end of the street.
You feel pleased with yourself, your guests can tell.
And they're glad to see you've got your sense of humour

back from the drycleaners. It's called taste, you tell them,
opening the wine, moving from person to person,
each one placed round the table in the right order.
You've gone to great lengths, *The Sultans of Swing*
insinuating. And then suddenly

your sister turns up without her husband, crying.
He's the most selfish prick she's ever known, she says.
You haven't seen her for five years, and here she is.
You say what you've always thought: 'Yes, you're right, he is.'
'Oh you rotten bastard' she says and leaves.

Your guests don't mention it, but something's changed.
Soon there's a strained atmosphere which even
your most highly-prized two-liners can't dispel.
One in the bush is worth two in the hand
if it's the right bush, you say. Everyone gapes.

Midnight, you sit in your kitchen and weep.
Your wife weeps too, but you don't comfort each other.

Forever Changed

You're tired, running a temperature, carrying
your empty medicine bottles to the dustbin.
The man you used to call dad hides behind it,
leaps out, boots you in the balls and face,
tips a bucket of piss over your head.
This happens every day, you're never ready.

Then you lose your job and all your savings
on a stupid bet. Your wife packs her bags,
takes the kids, moves to another country.
She's drilled holes in the radiators,
trampled avocados into the carpets
and warped your entire record collection.

The next thing you know you're beat up
and arrested in a dawn raid, charged with
possession of narcotics and firearms
and assaulting a police officer.
You're innocent but no one believes you.
Your lawyer washes his hands of you,

someone nails your cat to the door. Suddenly
you're getting letters of abuse, death-threats,
gift-wrapped substances that sting your fingers.
The postman tells you he hates you,
the milkman refuses to leave you milk,
people turn up to laugh and jeer at you

in the hairdresser's and supermarket,
follow you down the street throwing bottles
and rocks, dogs snapping at your heels.
The man you used to call dad kills himself,
leaves a note blaming you. Your novel
is dismissed as the ravings of a sick man.

Then every lover you've had publishes memoirs
in the Sunday papers, the details are awful.
Tuesday, you're photographed in a nightclub
with two fourteen-year-old girls and described
as a kinky pervert, a corrupter of youth,
a collector of soiled knickers.

Then your house is destroyed by fire.
Everything's gone, you don't even have one
photo of your kids' birthday parties left.
Your terrapins were boiled alive.
Your mother was asleep in the spare room.
Your wife hadn't renewed the insurance.

You wake in the night in a cheap hotel
to find you're deaf in your left ear,
have gone bald and have an ache
in the only two teeth you still bite with.
Then you're sitting at a bar looking scared.
A good Samaritan moves in to finish it.

Minus Three Point Six

Suppose there are three doors:
Religion, Insanity, Suicide.
Suppose you're on TV,
the hostess asks which door you'll take.
Suppose ten million viewers

and a studio audience of enemies
are all shouting their preference
and in the din the hostess mishears:
you ask for Religion, get Insanity.
You're shoved through and the door closes.

You try to shout for help, you want
to explain there's been a mistake,
you can't, can't move, feel as if
you're held in place by chains
or a pair of huge hands.

It's so dark you can't see yourself,
so quiet you could hear a plant move
though there are none moving.
There are no words in your head, just numbers.
You try but can't stop thinking about them:

One and one is two plus seventeen is eighteen
minus three point six is fifteen point eight
multiplied by twenty-seven point seven is
four thousand three hundred and sixty-five point six
divided by five point five is

Fingerprints

You hate the way the light-shade casts shadows
from a clear bulb. And now shiny black book covers
that pick up fingerprints. All you can smell
is boot polish and uniforms, the ink
on a statement you're supposed to have made.
You don't believe you said a word of it.
The door gets further away and isn't opened.

You're such a let-down, don't say the right things.
You wish you weren't who you are, aren't sure who.
There's a long line of men holding batons.
They'll rip your bollocks off, make you eat them.
They'll go at you till you believe everything
they tell you, you're the lowest of the low.
The door gets further away and isn't opened.

You crouch in the corner as the room shrinks
to the size of a crushed kneecap, small but
large enough to stick in your throat
from where a sound emerges, something like
a half-hearted prayer at a graveside
mixed with the sobs of genuine mourning.
The door gets further away and isn't opened.

Pathological

The director won't get out of his chair,
the caravan door's locked. Someone
knocks and asks if he's ready yet
two or three times an hour. There are
helicopters waiting, the police

have sealed off all the roads.
Leave me alone, the director whispers.
The last stages of something terminal
are all over the scene when he shoots it
three identical days later.

Government men follow him everywhere,
there's no hiding place. He crouches
in the shower, chanting. The water's
turned on full, his clothes are soaking.
He's trying to spot the microphone.

He goes for a paper, doesn't get back
for twelve weeks, can't say
where he's been. Doesn't know
a thing about it. He's twitching
like the beginning of a movie.

Keeping quiet like he's holding back
something big. No one suspects
his thoughts are of nothing.
He can shoot an apple off someone's head
or miss and not care less.

A House with Bare Floorboards

You peep through the upstairs window,
trying to figure out how much they know
behind the fence at the bottom of the garden.
You feel, you say, like a small child
is asking you questions in another language.

You've a tape that plays backwards
and sounds better that way, some apples
in a wooden basket: red, green, rotten.
I should ask why you took
the carpets up, cut them into pieces

about the size of table-mats,
crammed them inside plastic containers
and put them on the kitchen shelves.
Bare wood against bare feet, you say,
think I'll grow my sideburns again.

For a while now you've been well out of it,
believing in the existence of ghosts,
hardly daring to breathe or show your face.
It's good to have all that cleared up, you say,
to know the facts and nothing else.
You feel like laughing in the street
but don't want to make another mistake.

Now you're frowning, trying to remember
where you left your brown overcoat, afraid
you could have misplaced it for good.

Hannon in a Nutshell

His gripe was with the whole world, everyone,
and it seemed no amount of money
would put a smile on that long face.
His seventh album, called *Seventh Album*,
bristled with unresolved grievances,
'The Big Ships' and 'On The Other Hand'
the tracks that attracted most attention.
In the former, a solitary piano chord
repeated at five-second intervals
as Hannon grunted his ex-wife's name
was the sparest rock recording
since the heyday of Eight Nipples With An Attitude.
'On The Other Hand', on the other hand,
was its antithesis, a wild incantation
positively celebrating his loneliness,
the twenty-five percussionists
taking it into uncharted territory.
It is a stunning performance, shocking
as an amputation, twisted even, perhaps
completely paranoid, quite psychotic.

Hannon's mental decline over the following years
is well-documented elsewhere. Suffice to say
the Nixon Holiday Inn disturbance
was not an isolated incident
and the artistic output suffered correspondingly.
His relevance to the young of today
can be summed up thus: there but for the grace of God
could have gone your dad.

Three Mornings

You're waiting for the post,
nothing else is happening.
When it fails to arrive
you make a series of tapes,
your hundred favourite songs
by a hundred different artists.
It passes some twelve hours,

another seven and a half
listening back. By then
it's the morning, you're hanging on
for the post again, tired
but not sleepy. And surprised
how dull the songs sounded
the second time.

You apply for a job:
Head of Comedy
in a run-down comprehensive.
It goes to someone
who looks like Edgar Allan Poe
pretending to be Herman Melville,
a party-pooper for sure.

Then you're eating a pile
of toast. You watch
the postman walk past.
He's the same party-pooper
you saw in the dream.
His hair's a little
different, somehow.

Nobel Prize Poem

He awoke with no hangover
because he'd had no beer
and looked in the mirror.
He couldn't help noticing
that a box of old records
not worth listening to
teetered on his neck
in place of a head.
He tied his shoelaces.
He was barefoot.

*

At the time, he was seeing
a Scandinavian woman
whose life was her watercolours:
orange skies, pink highways.
She wanted to live in a cave
and win the Nobel Prize.
I'm not interested
in saving the world, he told her,
it's hard enough remembering
to change my underpants.

*

Then he wrote a story
about a bad writer
and thirty-seven people
sent him insulting letters:
How dare he portray them
in such a callous manner?
He couldn't even remember
meeting fourteen of them.
Three or four of them
were actually good writers.

Grey

It's not surprising he's gone a little grey
from the events of the past year or two,

only that he's not gone completely bald,
and he still can't believe he was ever

ridiculous enough to fall in love with her.
She turned him into the sort of man

who takes a packet of ham sandwiches
to work in a briefcase, one who sneers on the bus;

a man who feels like a book no one publishes
or an event history doesn't record.

*

She's like the knife-thrower's calm assistant,
she knows this much at least about the place she's in:

It's better than being buried up to your neck
with a bag of snakes tied over your head.

Her husband sounds completely furious,
something about his childhood and *it's not funny*.

She's noticed he laughs at different things.
In fact, he rarely laughs at anything

and this more than anything makes her laugh.
She starts after he leaves the room.

The Last Time I Saw Ernest Hemingway

he told me all bad writers were in love
with the epic, punching me in the ribs.
It was the sort of thing I'd got used to
after the twelfth drink. This was the same night

Steinbeck dropped in to introduce himself.
'No chin son of a bitch' Ernest shouted,
'I'm a better goddamn writer than you...'
and bit the neck off a whiskey bottle.

In some biographies, he breaks a stool
over his head as well, but I was there
and this didn't happen – so much that's said
about him's bull. Something not so well known

is that the CIA were onto him
for supporting Castro. 'That's one' he said,
pointing to some squarehead drinking tonic,
and for the first time in our long friendship

I knew Ernest Hemingway was frightened.

Star Guest of the Day

Everybody's laughing
about this comedian

who's been found guilty
of blackmailing himself,

though I prefer his
semi-serious roles,

like *Jackson*, who trims
his wife's pubic hair,

suggests she puts it
in a pie for him.

He was also good in
A Pile of Babies

And A Pile of Sand,
where he tells Cockwormer,

the bookmaker who loves him,
'They wish they had my head

in a noose. They have. My legs
are starting to tremble

like a house For Sale board
in a hard wind.' His face

is a blank domino
under a table

among a group of boots
that need polishing.

Eye, Lips, Miss

He was out of his head for a long time,
moving from place to place, making few friends,

behaving like a minor character
in an unwritten country 'n' western number.

These days he hardly goes out of the house.
He's got everything he needs right with him.

He flicks through photographs of his ex-wife,
chooses the prettiest, pins it to the dartboard.

He hasn't rinsed his coffee cups in years.
He throws the darts: nose, eye, miss, chin, miss, eye

Five Years

Easy to see what had gone against him
now it was finished. He'd sit in the dark

mulling over all their conversations.
He remembered them down to the last 'er'.

There was so much he needed to get right.
He could never run out of stuff to add.

Music filled the room but missed him
and he'd fall asleep in the chair and dream

he was a city where everyone lived alone
in buildings that resembled smokers' lungs.

Eccentric Hair

There was something grinning on the telly:
Everything's creative, it said, meaning
staring at a shadow on the ceiling.
I didn't switch off, just sort of grunted.
I wasn't good for much at the time
except worrying about the first post
coming ten minutes after the second,
the cop who parked outside my house reading
How The CIA Murdered Bob Marley
and the gangsters who tailed me when I went
to the bank, to the shops, to the dentist.
I was low, listening to the same song
over and over: *Don't Tell Me You Don't Believe It*
& Call Yourself A Friend
and I'd no idea what I wanted,
other than to be able to relax
and see the funny side of things again,
maybe think back to being seventeen,
wishing I was Bob Dylan or someone
or at least had pretty eccentric hair.
I just needed to get out more, out of the house.

My suit was at the drycleaners so I wore jeans
and a denim jacket. I leaned against the bar
avoiding the eyes of the other customers:
the place was full of all the fools I'd ever been.
I heard them getting more and more maudlin.

Lingerie on a South Yorkshire Clothes Line

1

Thirty-five years old and it was looking
like he'd always be a virgin. A woman once gave him

a short lift in her car
but it was a long time ago, they hadn't kept in touch.

Another time, stuck at a train station
in deep snow, just him and someone called Sue

huddled in front of an electric fire
in the waiting-room all night... maybe

she'd been married, he couldn't remember,
only the way her pale skin flushed.

Women were just pictures in magazines,
that was the way he tried to look at it.

He'd plenty of women, more than he knew what to do with.

2

Six pairs of knickers from next door's clothes line.
And a camisole top. He denied it

but the girl's brother thumped him anyway.
Well he was a weirdo, guilty or not.

His secrets included a pair of eyes
tattooed on his bell-end.

He'd been sixteen. The tattooist
who'd got him drunk and talked him into it

was arrested some years later, back of The Ship,
sucking off anyone who wanted it.

He'd put the tattooist out of his mind,
as much as was physically possible.

3

Eleven paperback novels,
including *Goldfinger*. And all the magazines

in heaps around the room,
torn-out pages sellotaped to the walls.

Bedclothes, unwashed for months.
A whip he'd used to thrash himself.

No mail. No address book
or note. No one to be informed.

A pint pot containing
nine pounds forty-nine pence in twos and ones.

III. DON'T WORRY

Don't Worry

A man in the Elephant and Castle
said there were games I should know more about,
I should try fags on the backs of my hands
or taking a shotgun to bed with me.
I recalled him dropped in the street one night,
the fine crack in his skull, the blood, the cold,
the copper who didn't think he'd make it.
'I tell thee lad, listen, what I don't know
about masturbation's not worth knowing.'
The place was suddenly brighter, I realised
I wasn't visible, he wasn't talking
to me at all. His brother came in then
with the news Clothes Line wouldn't be coming,
they'd been in a crash, all their fucking gear
was written off. A girl who followed them
from gig to gig began to shake her head.
'Don't worry' I told her, 'no one was hurt
except the bass player. His ribs showed through
his blood-soaked shirt as they tried to free him
from the snare drum.' I drank up and set off
along the canal, kicking at loose stones,
whistling one of the old songs I'm sick of,
sometimes stopping to see if I could spit
hard enough to reach the opposite bank.

Untitled, South Yorkshire, Mid-Eighties

1

When we get to The Wop
the barstaff are mopping up blood
and though it's only twenty past ten
the shits won't sell us a drink.
Except for a few hairies
clinging to pint glasses by the juke-box
the place is empty anyway.
It seems some smartarse in a suit
looked at one of the Angels
the wrong way, so they held him down
on the floor by the bar
(where the barstaff are now mopping)
and removed all his teeth –
'With a pair of pliers, and no
anaesthetic' says the landlord.
We talk him into selling us
a Guinness carry-out, he's not
too bad a bloke. Motorhead
have been in town, their fans
are all over the place
and on the train, grunting like apes.
One of them tosses off in the aisle,
looking up at the security camera
till someone else pulls it down
and starts a game of rugby with it.
Everyone is laughing.
A man with a glass eye
sits down next to me and tells me
I'm Nigel Fisher, child murderer
just out, and John turns round
and asks if he wants his eyes
to match. He looks
sort of startled, moves to another seat
– runs like a scalded bear
when he sees us getting off behind him
in Wombwell. Some miners
have overturned a police car

outside the Prince of Wales
and kicked the coppers unconscious.
Coppers are everywhere,
assaulting just about anybody.

2

Terry's drinking Newcastle Brown,
his right arm in plaster.
He's charged with threatening behaviour
and resisting arrest
but reckons the coppers haven't a case
and *he* ought to charge *them*.
After all, he says, he was only
fetching the paper and a bottle of milk.
We wonder about John, disappearing
without telling anyone anything.
Mr Barker weeps at the bar,
both his sons under arrest,
given terrible kickings.
People just ignore him.
The place is almost empty anyway.
Sam tells us about a snowman
built round a concrete post,
wearing a copper's helmet,
and some copper who drove fast
into it to flatten it
and is still on the sick, probably.
A woman with a broken arm
sits down at the next table with
a woman with a broken leg.
Sam's guilty of threatening behaviour.
Bound over, which prevents him picketing.
He's signed for the few hundred pounds
he'll pay back ten or twenty times
over the next four years, says
all the other people in the queue
wore bandages and plaster casts.
It was a big queue, one of the biggest.
A pale youth approaches, selling
SUN-FREE-ZONE stickers for the fund.

3

The off-licence and chippy
both go bust, it's a long walk
if you want anything now.
John writes from Bournemouth:
he's working in a health-food shop,
isn't coming back
till the strike's over
and the coppers gone.
George Barker shows everyone
his black and swollen balls.
His eyes seem to have grown wider,
taking over his face.
Two thousand coppers in armour
get one man into work at Cortonwood,
a convicted robber-with-violence.
A funny thing happens
on the way to Nottingham
only it's not really
Nottingham but Kettering
and it's not really funny.
Be careful what you say,
the phones are tapped
and the man from *The Mail*
is looking for a good story,
that's him at the foot of the stairs.
Two coppers perjure themselves
but contradict each other
and Terry's found not guilty.
Fucking coppers, says a bearded man
from the Socialist Workers' Party
in a loud voice to nobody.
The place is almost empty.
If he's not a copper
then I'm Gabriele D'Annunzio.
Someone switches the telly on.
Oh aye, says Terry, who's that then?
Bob Geldof asks for donations:
the starving Africans, etc.

Hyphen

The party was like the hyphen in Seymour-Smith.
The men were a stiff bunch, the women even worse.
I ended up pretending I'd the shits:
'Must have been the meat, I'm not used to it.'
We needed great mouthfuls of air, walked rather than
take a taxi. Jeanette took her shoes off
and her feet got dirty. She washed them in the sink
while I picked up a book. I read aloud,
it was pretty funny. You know the book I mean.
There was a lot of noise outside: dogs, screams
and Jeanette came and peered through the curtains,
leaving a trail of damp, talcumed footprints
which I pointed out when she turned back round.
'When are you going to get your clothes off?' she said.

Elsecar Reservoir

Although languid on the surface
Elsecar reservoir is dangerous
to swim in. Underwater currents
can grab and drag you down
into a system of potholes.

I hear myself say this
and can hardly believe it.
Jeanette turns away, startled.
Old people are feeding ducks,
a few fishermen sit still.

Pike are another reason
for not swimming, I say.
They've been known to swallow
whole men, boys anyway,
let's put it like this –

It's looking like rain
says an old man with a cap
and a dog that cowers.
It weren't forecast though
he adds as he passes.

Let's put it like this,
you definitely wouldn't want
to go swimming with the fuckers.
I stop and sit on the bank,
feeling in my pocket for my fags.

One of the fishermen pulls in
a strange object, nothing
like a fish. Everyone
stands around discussing it
as it flip-flops on the bank

then suddenly it's down the bank and gone
before anyone can stop it.
Two girls aged four and six
start to cry in the next street.
We can hear them clearly

till the brass band starts up.
That's funny, Jeanette says,
I can hear a brass band
but I can't see it.
Seventy-Six Trombones is what they play.

Jerome K. Jerome

Saying that *Three Men in a Boat*
was written by W. Somerset Maugham
drops my standing in The Milton
on a busy quiz night.

Two men and their shovels
are on the steps outside as I leave.
I remember them from the park.
One forces a fart as I pass.

In Phil's Butchers

They're sure they know me from somewhere:
'Aren't tha t' bloke that rode naked
on a bike through Jump for charity?
Thi picture wa' in t' Chronicle.'
The previous customer leaves, coughing
something red and green onto the pavement.
'That's a poorly mister, dead on 'is feet 'e is.'
One of them decides he worked
with my brother at Johnson's
though I've no brother who worked there.
'Are tha sure?' he wonders.
An older man (is it Phil?)
pops his head in from the back room:
'Leave t' lad alone 'n' gi' 'im 'is pies.'
I hold them in my hand as I say 'Ta-ra'
and leave, taking off my dark glasses.
There's a patch of blue sky
where my eyes should be, which startles
an old woman crossing the road.
'By' I say, to reassure her,
'it's cold enough for a walking stick.'
'All laughter is despair' she replies,
'it's t' human condition, like.'

Refused Water

I said I'd paint the old couple's ceilings and walls
and now I am, in old clothes and with sheets
over the furniture. So much of it:
a double-bed, three armchairs, two sideboards, sofa.
You wouldn't think it's all that large a room either.

George keeps popping in to see how I'm getting on,
tells me all about himself, like the time
he walked it from Barnsley to Huddersfield,
it must have been 1927, he'd be eighteen.
He knocked on a door to ask for water

and was refused. He laughs at what he says
and I laugh too, perched like a Marx Brother
on top of the old, wobbly step-ladders.
Then a low shout from the next room
pulls his head round: Elsie, after the stroke.

George reckons she loves it, bossing him round:
build the fire up, do the washing and the shopping
and tidy up, make a cuppa, fetch the paper.
He never thought he'd end his days as a male nurse.
We've been married sixty-one years, he says.

I move the bed, uncover Elsie's loo.
George must have to help her on and off.
I push it back out of sight, get cracking.
He must wipe her, clean her, dispose of everything.
When the first coat's on I join them, say yes

please to a cuppa which I make myself.
The kettle takes an age to boil.
The kitchen is cold and dirty, too small.
I'll be old before long, with a kettle.
I hear Elsie asking George if it looks all right.

Remembering Dennis's Eyes

He always blinked too much,
like an overnight guest who leaves
with the toilet paper in his holdall
or leaves a dry blanket
covering a wet bed.
Even with the balaclava
turned round to hide his face
I could see him blinking
through the makeshift eyeholes.

Gimme the bastard bag
he yelled, tugging at it.
The iron bar bounced on
the guard's helmet five times
before he fell to his knees,
another four or five before
he lost his grip on the bag.
You saw nowt, *nowt*, Dennis hissed,
pinning me to the wall
with one hand, waving the bar
like a conductor with the other.

The last time I saw him,
years later, years ago,
he'd just tried to kill his ex-wife,
had been stopped by
his ten-year-old daughter.
He was running toward Darfield
like a wind-up toy
with a pair of kitchen scissors
sticking between his shoulder-blades.

Two Bombs Are Better than One
(for Martin Stannard)

When I was younger I believed
that one day the Prime Minister
would have a slit

instead of a mouth,
tempting us to mail complaints
direct to his face.

I believed there'd be a just
and glorious war
every thirty minutes

and full employment
manufacturing arms
and legs for the wounded.

I thought everyone would know
the difference between
John Ashbery and John Ash

and a pile of sticks.
I thought people would care
about a pile of sticks.

I've heard it said
that when a man drops bombs
on soldiers, he's doing it

from the goodness of his heart.
I've heard it twice, not once.
Maybe it was more than twice.

The Next Move
(for Jim Burns)

Think I'll write a story
about a nice young man
who through no fault of his own
becomes a werewolf.

Think I'll write a story
about someone who won't leave the house
on Friday the thirteenth
and gets electrocuted by their kettle.

Maybe one about someone
who won't leave the house
except on Friday the thirteenth
would be more interesting.

Death's Boots
(for Ian McMillan)

In a previous incarnation, I climbed mountains
and sang my own praises, anticipating the trend.

On each wall of my home hung gaudy self-portraits.
I was posing for the camera before I invented it.

Then I was told I was a fool, that my career was over
for perfecting the ever-lasting light-bulb.

So I took a post kicking the oats out of farmers.
The money was good. Death's Boots, they called me.

I became involved because I saw no reason not to.
The reasons would pile up later like wood-shavings

from the pencils of the man who wrote *The American Century*.
That man was me, Death's Boots.

Eternal

Little nobodies
with big ideas
– don't think about them,
think about the woman
who'll be home soon,
who'll cross the room
in purple French knickers,
her navel deep enough
to slurp white wine out of.

Sheep, the (ha! ha!) eternal sentinels.

Outside, someone starts
strumming a guitar, badly.
The things people will do
to try to get applause.
You turn the radio on
to drown him out:
Everybody's dying
and some fool's singing about it.

Sheep, the (ha!) eternal (ha!) sentinels.

Men Without Clothes

(for my Mother)

My mother says the young people across the yard
spend half their time running about naked.

They hold barbecues in the early hours
wearing nothing but glitter in their hair

and she has to tell them to be quiet
some people have to work for a living

and that they can't shock her: she used to be a nurse.
They look so daft, she says, men without clothes.

My father rustles the paper: How long will dinner be?
It'll be as long as it takes, my mother says.

The Only Son at the Fish 'n' Chip Shop

He lived with his mother till he was forty-five
and no one was allowed to touch his head.

He worked on a novel for twenty years
without writing a word. He didn't like people

who wrote novels. He often drank. One glass of beer
was too many, two glasses weren't enough.

Travel brochures were as far as he went.
A football match, one time. He often said

Why would anyone want to think about a potato?
He painted his door with nobody's help.

The Visit

The only song he plays is 'What's in it for me?'
and I can't listen to it for too long

before I want a bucket to put over my head.
He asks how much I've made this year, how much

last year, how much I'll make over the coming year,
his voice sticking in my ears like an infection

nothing the doctor prescribes will clear up.
He has a pension plan, doesn't like me

spoiling his chance of getting value for money:
'You smoke too much' he says. And I do, in his house.

Experience

He's glad of his experience
when he comes up against the likes of Sam.
He's bought her chocolates, tickets, flowers
and now, Christmas in mind, a pair

of expensive binoculars. He reckons
they're his best chance of winning her
before she turns forty. He loves her
record collection, similar to his own

only better, and she makes
a great chilli. He's learned
from past mistakes – you've got to give
women time to get used to the idea.

I wish him luck, as he lopes off
to the toilet, returning with
a packet of liquorice condoms
he waves across the table: 'Just in case.'

The Laughing Face

I think I've reached the age
where I become resigned
to certain things,
like my lack of interest
in almost everything
nearly everyone else
gets worked up about.
Like my own obsessions, this stuff
the least obscure of them.

I'd hate to be buried
while still breathing.
It could happen
without me noticing,
leave me with nothing
to look forward to
except the loss of consciousness.
It could have happened already,
or be happening right now.

Pretending things are fine
gets to be a habit.

Some people live longer
than they wanted
but never long enough.
They go deaf, have no one
to talk to, the lucky ones.

Encounter

The moment his mouth opened to say 'Hi'
was like a century of crass American heroes
and their effect on successive generations,
meatheads who cry into their beer at the drop of a coin,
the first incessant whine that comes along.
Maybe I should have screwed him up, put him in my pocket.
Instead, I bent over backwards not to stir up trouble.

Time passed slowly as he dragged me from pub to pub,
talking as if love had never been made,
which was also the way he walked. His tattooed lip
gave him the look of a thug not to be messed with,
it became unclear to me how we'd ever met.
I knew nothing about him, only that he was different
to any other psychopath I'd got drunk with;
for one thing, he was more likely to weep at odd times,
looking at me as if there was something
I could do or say to help, as if I would if I could.

Spock's Brain

The best start to this year
would be to make a vow
and break it the minute
my head clears, something about
getting myself ship-shape,
sorted out. I'm not sure
if I'm drinking tea or
coffee or something else
but at least it's liquid.
When I pick up the paper,
I'm entitled to not
like what I see, or laugh
if there's anything funny
or not to laugh at.
I can raise my bushy
eyebrows all I want to,
make a face once or twice.
Sit here in my shirtsleeves
like a sane man who still
hopes things will get better.

Now I'm watching *Star Trek*,
an episode in which
Spock's brain is stolen,
leaving Kirk and the rest
less than forty minutes
before *Greece on a Tenner*
to search the galaxy,
find the brain and put it back
so Spock can say 'Thank you'
politely but coldly.

Meeting Hudson

The holes in my teeth, and the broken bits,
can get to my concentration
at bad times. I'm ordering
at the beer festival, forget
and simply point, ending up with
Kelsall's Brainwhacker.
At the back of my head
I hear a woman say
'Mark's been busy with the new patio.'
I look round: Where is Hudson?
I've thirty pounds for him
burning a hole in my pocket.
I take my mind off it
with the great North Minnesota bank raid
of 1876. A few
liberties with the facts
were taken in *The Long Riders.*
I've cramp in both legs
but ignore it.

Whining, Cascading

You've spent days making tapes
so you can sell the records
for whatever you might get
which won't be much
but better than nothing.
Now your head's a compilation
of whining guitar solos
and cascading drum-breaks,
making it hard to think.
Not that you want to think.

The post. You've won
a cash prize. It could be
anything from five hundred
to sixty thousand pounds, or
it could be £1.
If you fill in the form
authorising your bank
to debit £9.75 a month
the cash prize will be sent to you.

Back from the supermarket
with some shopping, you find
a free wristwatch inside
the packet of tea-bags.
It occurs to you
you could buy the whole lot,
stock up with enough tea
to last a couple of years,
then stand on a corner
and sell the watches.
But you don't have enough
capital to cover
the original investment.

Not California

Time passes slowly here in South Yorkshire.
The dustbin men came yesterday. Maybe
it was the day before, the day the couple
passed the house and had this conversation:
'What do you mean, I'm the one that's to blame?'
'You're the one that's to blame, that's what I mean.'
They said this three times, then they were out of
my life for ever.

Something I've never done is fly a hang glider.
I'm embarrassed about so many things.
I'm lazy, a weakling, can't even stop smoking.
My cough gets on my nerves but at least I own it.

So much for the jolly version.
On this binge I'm flat on my back
on the living-room floor, too smashed
to unlock the door for my wife.
She's shouting my name, banging the window,
looking at me as if to say
It's three in the afternoon, for God's sake
what are you up to?

She's back at ten. I'm still flat out of course, and wake
slowly, unsure where I am, hearing the tapping
at the window without understanding.

This is a small room. It's true it could be smaller.

Praying for a Miracle

I'm walking down Cherry Tree Street
in the early afternoon
of my fourth day without a smoke.
The wet roofs seem wrongly-set
to the houses, as if they might
slide off at any moment.
A landscape shaped by subsidence
where a man in a leather jacket
uses a small cup to bail rainwater
from a purple fibre-glass topless beach-buggy.
Hey, he shouts, cigarette smoke
all over him, don't I know thee?
I think not, I cross the road, I go in
an off-licence and stand behind
two girls spending twenty pence
on a variety of small sweets,
taking their time, changing their minds
then changing them back, making
the fat young man behind the counter
sigh. He wants to watch the snooker
on the small black-and-white TV
in the doorway behind him.
He has a stool there to sit on,
and an open can of beer
and smoking cigarette on a shelf,
and I turn round and walk out
without buying cigarettes or anything.
The beach-buggy has a nameplate:
Helter Skelter. On the side.
I'm an hour or hour and half
from the place where I can shake
the money-tin, rattle the coins.
It'll sound good, like more.
It'll sound like wealth, enough
to start a new life with.

Half Deaf

If I'd never listened to music on headphones
and drank all night, I'd be a different person,
either the village idiot
or the most desperate man you'd ever set eyes on.

With Nothing But A Brick Wall To Look At (And My Eyes Shut),
that's the name of that song. I could have got well drunk
in the time it's taken to remember.
All I had to go on was the harmonica solo.

I only hear half of what I believe.
I understand it could be like this for some time.
I need a holiday, have to settle
for pinning postcards to the walls instead.

Swamp Music

The band are starting up in the corner.
They're called Swamp Music: two lead guitarists,
a lot of hair. The vocalist
looks like he did three years on a chain gang
or do I only want to believe that?
He can't sing but the band are as good as they get

for Barnsley – I'm grinning, can't stop.
This is the place someone threw a pint glass,
missing Terry's head by inches, denting the wall
so deep I'm sure it would have been fatal.
I wasn't there, but saw the dent later.
Terry showed me, wide-eyed with something like wonder.

Reckless

I called to make contact
with someone still living, he says.
You're just hungover, I tell him,
pull yourself together.
No, he says, I've passed out
at too many parties.

Now we're off to a football match.
He always drives too fast. We cross the line
and head straight at a transit van,
Lynyrd Skynyrd on the cassette,
sounding muted
with just one speaker working.

Something Unfixed

There's nothing insulting
about the rain,
it's everybody else
owning cars
makes me feel insulted,
walking back from the shops
with plastic bags
cutting into my fingers
and my shoes leaking.
Today's insults
already include
hearing that homelessness
isn't a tragedy,
merely unhappiness,
and it's not even ten a.m.
I pass a man who wishes
he could afford to go
to the dentist, another
whose wife is
deteriorating.

The Persuaders

A well-known nobody
is opening The Countryman in Wombwell
and some people are ridiculous enough
to turn up and ask for his autograph.
He's ridiculous enough to sign them.
Twenty years on, we sit arguing

over who it was: Tony Curtis? Or
Roger Moore, before he was James Bond?
The beer's warm and a rockabilly band
are trying to pretend electricity
hasn't been invented. The harmonies are great
if you like that kind of thing. When we leave

the six of us walk in single file
up the narrow street that takes us
past The Angler's Rest and The Ship
and the Conservative and Catholic clubs
and British Legion and Royal Oak
and The Alma and Little George
and into the Horse Shoe,
where the barmaid is a comedienne:
'Good evening, ladies and beasts.'
It's Nev's round.